DISTRACTED GEOGRAPHIES
AN ARCHIPELAGO OF INTENT

... the sombre strategies of the terrain.
Night, snow, and sand make up the form
of my thin country,
all silence lies in its long line,....

—PABLO NERUDA,
'Discoverers of Chile'

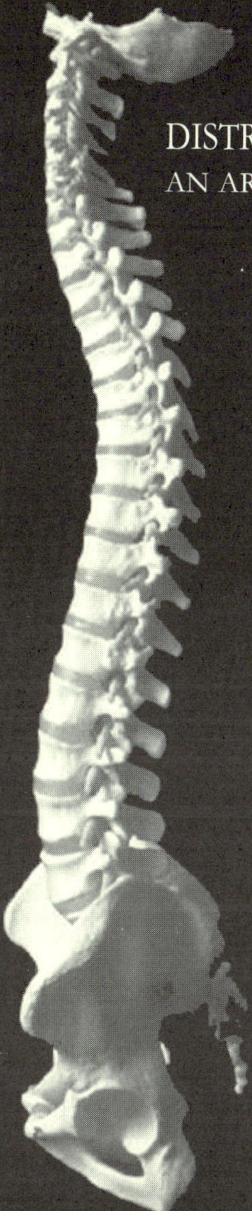

DISTRACTED GEOGRAPHIES

AN ARCHIPELAGO OF INTENT

Sudeep Sen

WINGS PRESS

Published by Bryce Milligan for
Wings Press
627 East Guenther, San Antonio, Texas 78210. U.S.A.
milligan@wingspress.com
www.wingspress.com

Distributed in the United States of America
by Small Press Distribution [and Wings Press]
www.spdbooks.com

Cataloguing in Publication Data
Sen, Sudeep, 1964—
Distracted Geographies: An Archipelago of Intent
I. Title; II. English Poetry/Fiction;
III. Scotland/UK; IV. India; V. World Literature
821'.9'14

ISBN 0-930324-95-1

Graphic Designer: Subrata Basak of Desire Design
Typeset in Garamond 12 pts.

First Edition

for
Aria

CONTENTS

I

FOREWORD
MEMORISED FRAGMENTS

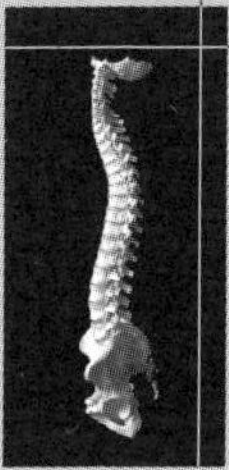

In the great square
The prolonged vowel of silence
Makes itself plainly heard.

DOM MORAES, 'Absences'

Poetry is preparation for death.

NADEZHDA MANDELSTAM

It is one thing to sing the beloved. Another, alas,
to invoke that hidden, guilty river-god of the blood.

RAINER MARIA RILKE, 'Duino Elegy 3'

Air, that's colourless in its core, seems, given
a landscape, blue-very often even
dark blue.

JOSEPH BRODSKY, 'Eclogue V: Summer'

For thousand years I have walked this earth's passage
by day and night — from Lanka's shores to Malay's vast seas.
I've travelled much — been a guest at Bimbhishar and at Ashok's courts,
stayed in the distant nights, in the town of Bidharba.
I'm long worn-out; around me waters of sea and life have endlessly swirled.
My only peace — a fleeting moment snatched with her —
Natore'r Banalata Sen.

Like the dense ink-night of Bidhisha, her hair — black, deep black;
her face—like the delicate-weave of Shrabasti's filigree-frieze.
Just as a lost boatman, rudderless, tossing in the far seas
chances upon a lush-green Isle of Spice,
I too caught a sight — saw her, a mere glimpse in the dark. Gently, raising
her eyes, she whispered: "Where *were* you, all this while?"
[And there she stands at my dream's end — my own Banalata Sen].

With soft-settling hiss of dew, evening closes the day's end;
kites erase from their wings, sun-stain smell of flight.
When colours of the earth gently fade, fireflies light up their palette,
and old songs find new lyric, old stories new score.
Birds return home, so do the rivers; as life's trade — its give-and-take — cease.
Only the dark stays. And just as it remains, so does sitting by my side,
face to face, my own Banalata Sen.

—JIBANANANDA DAS, 'Banalata Sen'
Translated from the Bengali by Sudeep Sen

II

INDOORS/OUTDOORS 1
GARTINCABER, DOUNE

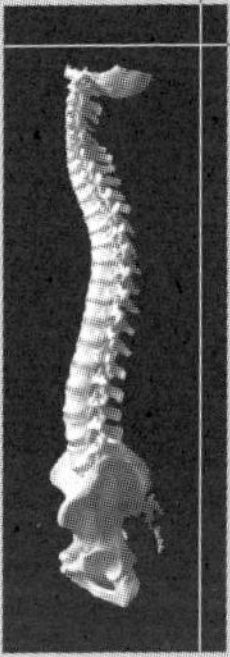

There stands death, a bluish distillate
in a cup without a saucer. Such a strange
place to find a cup: standing on
the back of a hand.

RAINER MARIA RILKE, 'Death'

Lighter than air
than water
than lips / light light
Your body is the footprint of your body

OCTAVIO PAZ, 'Transit'

1

My thin country,
  my own spine.

Locked dactyls,
  unconnected,

stretched,
  deeply fused.

* * *

Juices spill
  cautiously

like preserved
  semen

anguishing
  to let go.

* * *

Haemorrhage
  underlying

my retina
  focuses

incorrectly
  on the passion

of spent
  moulting skin.

* * *

Steel splinters
  injecting metal

hold
  fragile bones,

desire
  a delicate touch.

2

She feels lost
  in this wild

peace
  of nature.

The sequoia
  tree, twisted

in its intent,
  fans out

green fir.
  Proud

pine-needles
  prick

the pain
  of sanity.

  * * *

My sight line
  skated

along the
  damp

grass-blade
  surface

outside.
  My pupil's

camera lens
  rack-

focused,
  adjusting

its vision,
  trying to

match
 the balanced

laws of
  physics.

The scene
  was unusual

and tropical.
  It was

the humid
  zone

of
  penumbra

I most sought
  out

and lusted
  after.

  * * *

Far away,
  the eyes of

a fox shone,
  drunk

in hunger.
  The greed

of flesh
  salivating.

  * * *

Ceramic
  still-life:

Coffee
  in my cup

cold
  with

neglect.
  An errant

wasp
  sniffing

around
  to mate,

perches
  itself

on the rim,
  parting

the pod
  of the

cup's floral
  disguise.

* * *

All sap
  refuses

custody
  of stained

invisible
  juice.

* * *

3

Radium

Pure liquid
  transgresses

proof
  of the spirit

itself,
  and all

I see is
  fall-out.

Atoms split,
  radium

spread
  in insidious

balmy blots,
  plasma

arrested
  on canvas oil,

permanently
  gelling

shapes in deep
  crimson,

blue, and
  pure white.

Undulations —
  transform

the sex
  of paint itself.

* * *

Radio-active
  chlorophyll

glitters in
  the wet

infused
  after-glow.

Grass-blades
  gleam

and show off
  their

slaughter-
  swathe

edge,
  defying any

trespasser's
  intentions

in clear view.
  Blood's

fluorescent
  dreams,

unsuited
  for this

clean
  rural air,

atomise and
  ignite,

sparking
  a steady

nuclear
  ambition.

* * *

The rolling
  Highland's

calm presence
  provides

some sanity.
  Its caché

bursting
  with

plenitude and
  produce—

wheatish-gold,
  ready,

upright, and
  confident —

still cows
  under

the weather's
  dictates —

dappled
  sunshine,

stippled
  rain —

a checkered
  history

of fertility
  and space.

* * *

Amid nature's
  safety

and its unwritten
  history,

lies
  unrestored,

a fifteenth
  century

mansion —
  'Gartincaber' —

its walls
  breathing life

into new
  occupants' exile.

Their displaced
  lives,

like the mansion's
  drive,

disappear into
  the open

country's hope
  and chance.

* * *

At the drive's
  end—

a graveyard—
  old and

overgrown,
  its plinth

still
  resuscitating

the past's
  presence.

* * *

4

Graveyard

The row of
  tall firs

guard life
  against

death,
  fact

from
  secret.

An avenue
  of arched

light—
  its emerald

glow filtering
  through

the matrix
 of branches,

its hypnotic
  marrow—

sucks me into
  its tunnel.

Wading
  through

the semi-
  tropical

green air,
  I stumble

onto an old
  graveyard,

its disused
  space

guarded by
  a wrought-

iron fence
  and lock,

its mettle
  buried

under the
  sanctity

of granite
  and

head-stone.
  Cryptic

nomenclature
  stating

names and
  dates

reveal only
  neutral

mysteries,
  the rest

choose
  to hide

under brown
  and green

of soil
  and leaves.

The only
  sounds:

the crackle
  of twigs,

hush of a
  freshly-lit

fire,
  the grace

of silent
  breeze,

my feet's
  shuffle,

tin-scratch
  breath of

my frayed
  lungs,

and the
  dead's

living
  heart-beats.

* * *

III

INDOORS/OUTDOORS 2
ARCHIPELAGO

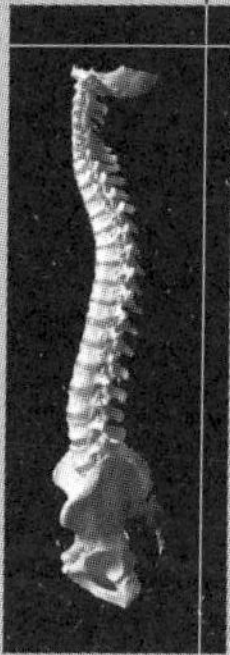

At the end of this sentence, rain will begin.

DEREK WALCOTT, 'Archipelago I':
Map of the New World

5

The unmapped
  shores

of the *loch*
  wanted

to warn us
  that

its variant
  levels

were just as
  deceptive

as the
  dense

[un]predict-
  ability

of the *haar*—
  the hoar-frost's

thick, thick-
  white.

* * *

The opulent
  verdure

was almost as
  oppressive

as the
  freshness

of water's
  aquamarine

glass
  and flower's

bee-stung
  petals,

as colour
  bled

profusely,
  incarnadine

and
  helpless.

* * *

It was humid,
  and

the sticky
  heat

tempted
  the clouds

to change
  their sex

from white
  to ash.

Rain was
  imminent.

6

She sniffed
  the

heavy air
  to taste

its bouquet
  and

strength.
  And all

of a
  sudden,

she lit up
  at the

scent
  and want

of wild
  mushrooms.

With the angled
  precision

of a Prague
  soprano,

her balletic
  fingers

picked
  the fruits

of deep
  taste—

piercing
  her nails

to test its
  inherent

danger and
  delicacy—

caressing
  the soft

supine stalk
with love,

translating
them

from one state
to another.

* * *

Taste
is measured

only by its
intent

and the
after-taste

it leaves
behind,

and the
  long

lingering
  desire

for more
  and more.

* * *

IV

INDOORS/OUTDOORS 3
DISTRACTED GEOGRAPHY

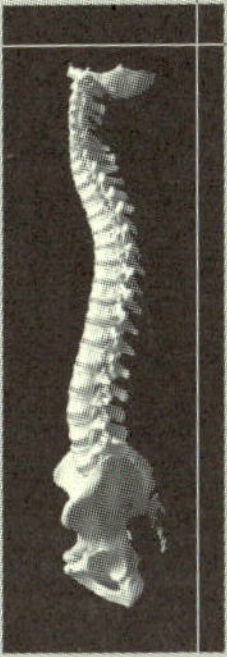

When the rain drives on the poppies they hold bright petals to the rain. From pew to pew we construct together geographies of a day: ....

DONALD HALL, 'To Build a House'

A kite's screech from atop a ruin:
Sign of rain.

ARVIND K. MEHROTRA, 'Bhojpuri Descant: XVI'

7

Rain started.
  Transparent

screen of angled
  water-fibre

connected
  the sky

to
  the new grass.

* * *

When the rain
  drives on

the poppies /
  they hold

bright
petals

to the rain.
From

pew to pew
we construct

together /
geographies

of
a day...

* * *

A rabbit
sat up,

startled
  as if

arrested
  in mid-coitus.

It must have
  liked rain

more than
  any pleasures

of body.
  Ears cocked,

it puffed out
  its small chest

to breathe in
  the wet.

* * *

After
  many hours,

the air
  cleared.

Morning mist
  that sat

dreaming,
  now lifted

its skirt,
  to

accommodate
  the want

of
  my eyes.

* * *

V

INDOORS/OUTDOORS 4
TROSSACHS

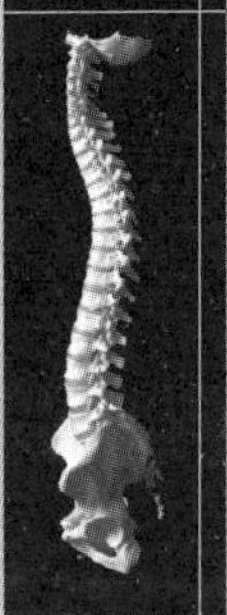

The skinny waterfalls, footpaths
wandering out of heaven, strike
the cliffside, leap, and shudder off.

Somewhere behind me
a small fire goes on flaring in the rain, in the desolate
ashes.

GALWAY KINNELL, 'Lastness'

8

I sat still,
  silently,

thinking
  only

of last
  night:

The perfect
  turn-on —

recitation
  fluid

like flowing
  lava,

twisted like
  enjambments

manipulating
  fusion.

We all sat
  around,

sunk sloppily
  in the

brown velvet
  sofa.

The log-fire
  fanning

our taste-
  buds

spilling iambs,
  text-tumblings

recognisable
  only

to the
  hawk-eyed.

  * * *

Subtlety
  of a

freshly kissed
  tongue.

  * * *

Secrets
  hoarded

willingly
  in our

own
  private hearts.

9

The pathway
  outside

was mere
  gravel

and dirt.
  My steps

made moist
  uncomfortable

pug-marks
  in the

deceptive
  slippery terrain.

* * *

The terrain ...
  make[s] up

the form
  of my

thin country,
  all silence

lies in its
  long line[s.]

* * *

The highland
  road,

rolls
  and meanders,

wrapping around
  the belly

of the Trossachs,
  like

a belt of tarmac
  ribbon.

* * *

The skinny
  waterfalls,

footpaths
  wandering

out
  of heaven,

strike
the cliffside,

leap, and
shudder off.

Somewhere
behind me

a small fire
goes on

flaring
in the rain,

in the
desolate ashes.

* * *

The fresh air
was poison,

my lungs
  thriving

in the acid
  it contained.

* * *

VI

DISTRACTIONS 1

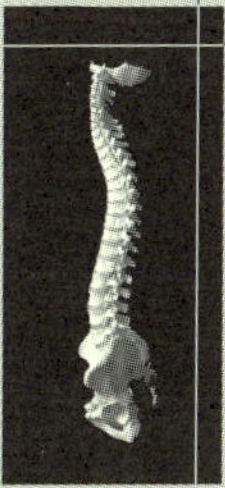

I am like sand in the hourglass
which can be time only in falling.
Ana Blandiana 'Condition'

broken glass is held together
with bits and pieces
of an old yellowed newspaper
Arun Kolatkar, 'The Cupboard: Jejuri'

There is no space
left in the diary. And the beads of quick
words scatter over his spouse's sepia-shaded face
adding the date in question like a mole to her lovely cheek.
Joseph Brodsky, 'A Polar Explorer'

10

Imagination I

Only
imagination,

memory,
pain,

and distractions
of humour,

keeps me
alive.

* * *

Sand Time

I am
like sand

in the
hourglass /

which
can be time

only in
falling.

* * *

Macallan

The single malt
explodes

from its husk,
swirling

in the cranium
of its own

shell,
flooding

my mind
  with images

that alternately
  switch

shutter speed
  and lens,

distilling
  sight,

whisking
  away

from the mundane,
  what is

absolute
  and essential,

and leaving out
  what is not.

* * *

Last Drop

I drink
  till

the very end.
  The last

drop
  evaporates

quicker than
  I could

possibly
  comprehend.

* * *

11

Tabula Rasa

I rid
  myself

of all
  clothes

I wear.
  I strip

all memory
  clean.

* * *

Imagination II

All I'm left
  with

is my fatal
  imagination,

the conjured
  dreams, and

a summer
  of metaphors.

* * *

Fission

That's all
  I really need.

Rest is
  uncontrolled

fission,
  pure passion.

* * *

VII

PASSION
Fifteen Movements on Erotica

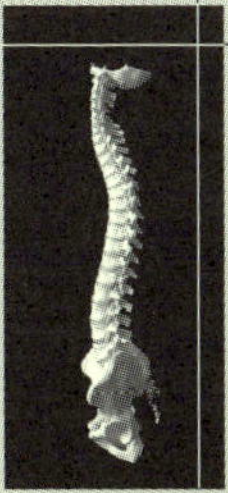

Images of your face
Bring me
The wild mane of summer leaves...
BEN OKRI, 'A Gentle Requiem'

the soft tumult of thy hair
JAMES JOYCE

I want
to do with you what spring does with the cherry trees.
PABLO NERUDA, 'XIV: Every Day You Play...'

12

Offering, Fluids

The kindness
  of libation,

lyric,
  and blood.

Her endless
  notes

left
  for me—

little secrets,
  graces,

trills
  recorded on

blue
  and purple

parchment
  to be lipped,

tasted,
  devoured—

only the
  essence remains,

its stickiness,
  its juice,

its
  memory—

* * *

Seamless
  juxtaposition—

the brute and
  the passion,

dry
  of the bone

and wet
  of the sea,

coarseness
  of the page

and smooth of
  the nib's iridium—

* * *

I try to
  trace a line,

a very long
  line—

the ink
  blots

as this line's
  linear edge

dissolves
  and frays —

like capillary
  threads

gone mad,
  twirling

in the deep
  heat

of the tropics —
  threads

unravelling,
  each sinew

tense
  with the want

of moisture
  and

the
  other's flesh.

* * *

There are
  no endings

here—
  only beginnings—

precious
  incipience—

translucent
  drops of sweat

perched
  precariously

on her collar-
  bone, waiting

to slide,
  roll unannounced

into the gulleys
  that yearn

to soak in
  the rain—

* * *

Heart-beat
  shift

the shape
  of globules

as they alter
  their balance

and colour,
  changing

their very point
  of gravity—

constantly deceiving
  the other—

* * *

I stand,
  wanting—

wanting
  more

of the bone's
  dry edge,

the infinite blur
  of desire,

the dream,
  the wet, the salt,

the ink, the rain,
  and,

the underside
  of her skin.

* * *

Images
  of your

face /
  Bring me /

The wild
  mane

of summer
  leaves...

* * *

Absences

Our mattress
  is the

ocean,
  the crushed

sheets,
  its waves.

We sail
  together,

full blown.
  But during

your long
  absences

as our vessels
  buoyant

on different
  shores,

the bed
  dreams:

I imagine,
  the wet

breaking
  the anchor

loose,
  defying current,

gravity, and
  electricity,

photons
  that propel

and burn
  even the wild

salted expanse
  into a monument,

a desire,
  permanent

like the ocean
  bed,

its pulses
  uncontrollably

rocking—
  the waters,

the bodies,
  the dreams.

* * *

Desire

Under
  the soft

translucent
  linen,

the ridges
  around

your nipples
  harden

at the
  thought

of
  my tongue.

You, arch
  like an

inverted 'c'
  move

yourself
  deliberately

wanting
  the warm

press of
  my lips,

its wet
  to coat

the skin
  that is

bristling,
  burning,

breaking into
  sweats of

desire,
  the sweet

juices of
  imagination.

But in fact,
  I haven't

even
  touched you.

At least,
  not as yet.

* * *

Lying Bare

Your bare
  stomach

is my pillow.
  When I

turn my head
  on one side,

warm air rises
  from

the valley
  to lull me.

On the other
  side,

you shield
  the sight

of your face
with

your bosom—
only to

devour me
in their gorge

near
your heart.

* * *

Taste

Our skin
breathes love

through
its pores,

the glands
  transforming

shivers
  into taste.

The taste
  of desire

is the taste
  of its warm

lingering
  after-taste.

* * *

Climax

Lips of
  a rose-

bud
  open

to let,
the dew

drop
in.

* * *

Release

The stamen
raises

its head,
bursting,

to shed
pollen:

relief-
rain

showers
  the

parched
  folds

of pink
  skin.

* * *

Morning

Buried
  in warm skin

toasted
  in the night's

passion,
  I struggle

this morning,
  to emerge

out of this
  heavy air.

* * *

13

Caress

Saryu,
  the Zen

poet wrote:
  Without

the brush,
  the willow

paints
  the wind.

To which
  I replied:

'Without
  the brush,

my breath
  paints

her
  bare skin'.

* * *

Kiss

A languorous
  kiss —

the faintest
  smell

of ocean—
  salt-lipped

breeze,
  pleading.

  * * *

Day Before
  Summer Solstice

We are sealed
  in marriage

today,
  to celebrate

tomorrow:
  the earth's

longest day.
  We are

mere stardust
  of an

ancient
  supernova,

one that gave
  us our

metal, blood,
  and breath.

* * *

Indian Dessert

Clumps
  of smoke

simmer
  in the pan,

and slowly
  lift

to caress
  the outline

of your
  breasts,

as you cook,
  stirring

the spices
  in carrot,

milk,
  and cream,

the ingredients
  that conjure

recipes
  of hunger

and passion.
  As you

stroke sugar
  and butter

and gently
  melt

toasted
  flakes of

grated
  almond-

shavings,
  more clumps

of perfumed
  smoke

permeate
  through

the silk
  of your shirt—

now
  transparent

in heat—
  painting

the outer
  circle

of the
  nipples

to an
  hardened

edge,
  tasting

the sweet
  skin,

the surface
  of the

crinkled
  base,

to a creamed
  mouthful—

an untampered
  delicacy.

* * *

Glued

Glued
together,

we lie
incurably

conjoined.
Just as

the sky and
the earth

are joined
by an

indeterminate
horizon,

so are we,
made one by

an indeterminate
  faith.

* * *

I want
  to do

with you /
  what

spring
  does /

with
  the

cherry
  trees.

* * *

VIII

INDOORS/OUTDOORS 5
Tower

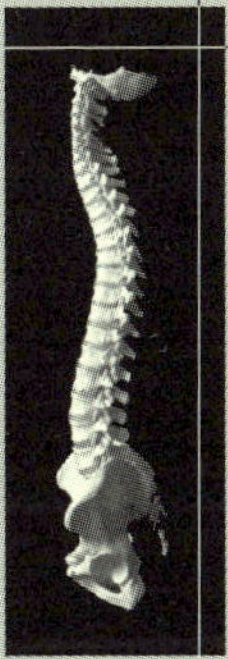

Every human being is a colony.
PABLO PICASSO

A low temple keeps its gods in the dark.
ARUN KOLATKAR, 'A Low Temple: Jejuri'

14

The tower—
  the *broch*—

its hexagonal
  mystery

couched within
  a cylinder

of incomplete
  spiral

stairways,
  its erect

stature,
  tempts us

to embrace
  its gothic

fragmented
  story.

  * * *

We walk
  towards

its height.
  It stands

on the unkempt
  green

that abounds
  in flocks,

sheep
  ready to

rub
  their wool

against
  us.

  * * *

There is
  something

uncomfortably
  friendly

about
  the approach.

First, a tame
  stray dog,

then sheep,
  and more sheep,

finally
  a barricade—

a row
  of stunted

trees,
  their mane

shaved-off
  in the wind,

a silhouette
  like

the bent pilgrims
  in

The Seventh Seal—
a static scene,

high
on the horizon.

* * *

We reached
the site.

A sign warned us—
the danger

of the tower
itself,

its tentative
life, and

its intention
to collapse.

15

But the swig
  of single malt

from
  our prized flask

fortified us
  for everything.

* * *

Peering around,
  high

like the tower
  itself,

we watched over
  the landscape

surrounded
  in the haze

of fading
  light,

our sight
  blurred

in the spirit
  of dusk air.

* * *

The secrets
  hidden

in stone
  and iron,

its vantage
  point

of
  days gone by,

kept a code;
  its lock

known only to —
  and hidden

within deceptive
  folds

of — the unveiling
  wind.

* * *

Medieval
  structures

have their own
  strictures,

their own
  rhythms,

their decrepit
  stance —

all there
  to distract

strangers
  like us away.

Like a false
  pass in a game

of chess:
  deftly castled

to alter
  geography,

to protect
  the lineage

of the monument
  itself,

from future
  map-makers

and hands
  of raping time.

* * *

Every
human being

is a
colony.

I too, am
a colony,

and
the coloniser.

* * *

16

Church Notes

An invisible
  song erupts.

I see myself
  in an

old church,
  where the

remnant tower
  was once

an elegant limb
  in the

structure's
  stone-proof

body. The choir
  picks up.

A swan-graced
  cellist—

her electric
  beauty set

in the pale
  of her youth—

swims in
  to steady

the waves. Her
  angelic

brows dip, as
  her right arm

travelling with
  the bow's polish

makes miniature
  Calder mobiles,

creating gentle
  short-lived

sketches
  in the air,

their impressions
  and

long languid
  lamentations

make her deep-
  oaked cello

breathe heavy,
  resuscitating

the congregated
  air

with secret
  notes

of libation—
  notes that

escaped from
  my hidden

postcard-stack
  I had

hoarded for
  years on end—

not knowing their
  implications,

or their desires.
  Now they

bloomed: magical,
  and perfectly

intoned. I ran
  into the tower's

inner temple.
  There was

no faith left
  in the apse—

only memories
  of slender

fingers stroking
  the cello,

the *chandipaat*
  baritone

invoking the myth
  of Durga's

incantatory
  verse-prayers

and images,
  scored

and inked
  permanently

by my script's
  roving italics.

* * *

It is morning
  again,

time to retire.
  I put my

night-gods
  to sleep.

Another postcard
  threatens

to arrive
  through

the door's
  letter-vent.

I am grateful
  for

the richness
  of

such meagre
  company.

* * *

17

I am alone
  here.

The vast country
  surrounds me,

closing in
  like

an advancing
  army.

* * *

I have no arms,
  they were

severed
  long before

I learned
  to write

or spell
  webs

of intricate
  delusions.

* * *

But I like it
  here,

I like being
  alone

in spite of all
  the clear light.

* * *

IX

EDINBURGH INTERLUDE

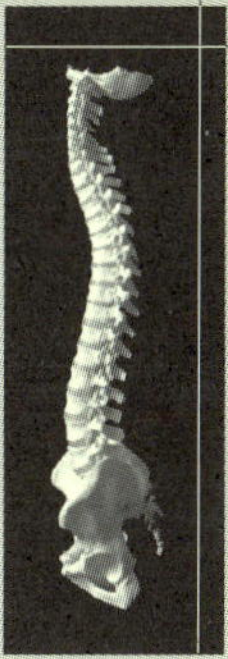

18

Ambassador

A friend
 who hoards

histories of
 Kolkata

in stories
 stored in

unpublished
 silos, spots

an Ambassador
 car,

an unlikely
 presence

on Edinburgh
  streets.

Scotland
  had never

before seen
  one

of its kind—
  its polite

Indian chassis.
  My own

desire
  to inhabit

its shell,
  its Bengali

carriage—
  affectionate,

gentle,
  rounded

and
  serene—

is to do with
  memories

of family
  and space—

mobile and
  expansive.

But what
  drew us

to
  its strength

and steel
  was its

unmolten
  wickedness,

its couched
  ambition

it quietly
  contained.

The body's
  reflection

in this sharp
  northern

light was too
  precious,

too clear
  for comfort.

The only
  respite —

untold tales
  recorded

in its
  unwarmed

motor,
  one that

now spills —
  imagined,

dreamt,
  gradually

unveiling
  its

uncoiled
  secrets

in high octane
  elasticity.

* * *

Asphyxia

I knew
  I was dying.

The cat-litter
  stink

that swept
  the well-

carpeted
  warmth

of suburbia,
  shed

all
  inhibitions.

Asphyxia
  choking me

even in my sleep,
  was made

to live
  forcibly

by allergy pills,
  of care.

Strange love
  it was,

feline
  to the core.

The hair's
  fine

invisible
  venom

let its
  autumnal

moult fall—
  follicle

rain-dust—
  stamping

dead,
  my sinuses.

But there
  was some relief,

an escape
  for both

me and
  the cats —

the kitchen
  window

kept open,
  reluctantly,

only due to
  a guest's request.

But it
simply let in

the owner's
fears—

anxiety
that

suburbia's
safe

oxygen
balance

may alter
or

loosen
their levels.

* * *

19

Three Heads at the National Gallery

Head I

My cranium
  stands

fossilised
  and

triangulated
  on the

black 'T'
  of a

crucifix.
  The blue

and white
  crescent

and head's
  hemisphere,

sit askance
  in their

bone-sharp
  intentions.

It was Breton
  who had

scripted
  the line-

breaks, and
  the cell's

own
  narrative.

[based on Pablo Picasso's *Head* (1913).
Paper collage, charcoal & pencil on card.]

* * *

Head II

My imagination
  is cupped

entirely in
  the creased

palms
  of my hands—

lepered, folded,
  and bronzed—

encased
  and colonised

within the anaesthetic
  clarity

of a transparent
  cube.

But don't
  you see,

it is trying to
  reach out—

to feel you—
  even though

it is only
  an imagination

of love
  contained

within heart's
  own sleeve.

[based on Pablo Picasso's *The Head or Arm with Sleeve* (1948). Bronze.]

* * *

Head III

Plasmic,
  the green amoeba

resembles
  my hair,

one that has
  collected silt

and humour
  for centuries.

My eyes, lips,
  cheeks, nostrils —

all pink
  in the white

semen of life.
  Only blue

provides me
  with hope,

and blue—
  and blue—

and death—
  and blue.

[based on Pablo Picasso's *Head* (1971).
Pastel on paper.]

* * *

20

JANUS AT THE BOOK FESTIVAL

Gulls

Gentle up-drift
  from the

Firth of Forth's
  sea-breeze

carried gulls
  all the way to

Edinburgh's
  downtown patch.

Instead of finding
  their usual

resting place
  in the park,

one that separates
  the old

and the new city,
  they chose

the white-tented
  Charlotte Square

this time. Perhaps
  they mistook

the white-gloss
  of the tent's

exterior
  as billowed

sails.
  They are loyal

visitors here,
  every August.

* * *

Saviour

I got lost
  several times,

got arrested on
  several counts,

but every time
  I was rescued

by my gull-friend,
  Janus. She had

an instinct
  for me, to find

me at the
oddest places,

then carry me
on her soft

feathery back,
and keep me

company through
up and down

of literary
living.

* * *

Flight

The gulls knew
when to arrive,

when to leave,
when to match

their flight-arcs
  with the cadence

of Gaelic
  lilts—

Humans have
  a long way—

Janus quietly
  disappeared,

merging
  with

the flock
  once again.

* * *

21

Cacophony

In the
  translucent

sheer of
  cacophony,

I make
  the clearest

sense
  of the world.

* * *

Baptism

In this empty
  featureless

apartment,
  I stand waiting

for my furniture
  to arrive.

The telephone
  rings —

you are the first
  to call.

The first call
  in a barren house

is propitious
  they say —

baptism
  by human voice.

Though my address
  has altered,

house changed, my
  telephone number

remains the same
  lest people

forget, to connect,
  me inside

this new space,
  with the world

outside. But this
  vacant room

reverberates
  your voice, and

mine, and
  many others,

like the bass-hum
  that lives under

the drum-skin,
  stretched

to its limit
  to relay moments

of quiet utterance—
  sacred—

not always
  understood

at the time
  perhaps — but

in deepest silence
  lie

the most powerful
  words.

* * *

22

Suspended Particles

Two shafts
  of sunlight

bisect
  this room,

as this
  well-defined

twin-track
  of silver-dust

floats,
  suspended

in the dense
  still air.

Outside,
  the traffic roars,

inside,
  the clock ticks

with well-
  intentioned

regularity,
  quite unlike

the random
  particles

that swim
  aimlessly

in slanted clear-
  cut columns.

A lost bee
  drones in

through
  the window

carelessly
  left ajar

to entertain
  this show,

its minute
  sting

picking
  every particle

it catches
  in its path,

as its
  translucent wings

caught against
  this light,

filter
  specifics

from randomness,
  to make sense

of it all.
  My own sight

trapped within
  my heavy eyelids,

detects
  the subtle beauty

of frenetic
  atoms,

the nuclear
  weight

weightless
  as air in space,

light as post-
  monsoon breeze.

But as the
  evening-

light pales,
  congregations

of silver-
  specks

make themselves
  invisible,

even though
  their presence

remains,
  alive

and
  whispered.

* * *

X

DISTRACTIONS 2

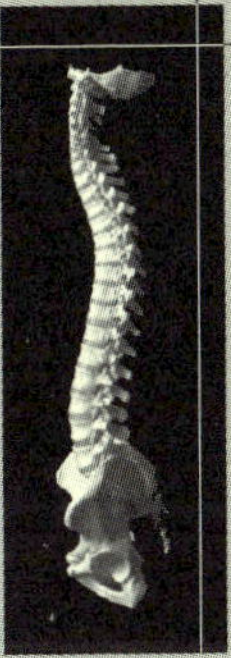

23

'C'

My eyes open,
then close.

Sleep slowly
melts

the pupil's
edge,

warning
my lashes

to firm up
and stand up

to the task
at hand.

It is only
a test

of vision,
a mere

sight-check,
all within

the aperture
of reason.

I had always
measured

my sight
by what

I could
not see.

So I never
wanted

perfect
  vision.

In the
  clinic's

darkened
  stage,

surrounded
  by lenses,

charts, and
  the doctor's

searching
  eye,

I smelt her
  instinct

for the
  raw senses.

At the time,
  I was

trying merely
  to read

a back-lit
  board

full of
  pasted

letters. Its
  law

of diminishing
  return

provoking
  pretences

only a soft-
  focus

lens could
  clarify.

The curve
  of

the doctor's
  breasts

matched
  the sweep

of the letter
  'c',

blurring
  in the

fluorescent
  distance,

the glow
  that only

partially
  repaired

my sight.
  The rest

of the story
  my

eye's matted
  screen

could gauge,
  projected

only a
  security

of imagination,
  one

that makes
  fantasy real,

perfectly
  visible

and viable,
  much like

the comfort
  inherent

in the
  gentle

curve of the
  letter ‘c’.

* * *

Havanas

Two unfinished
  Havana Cigars

lay
  side by side,

naked
  in the glass

and ash
  of last night.

This morning
  there was

something sombre
  about them,

perhaps
  a pact

that's only
  possible

when
  leaves are burnt

to their
  barest brown,

fired
  with the cough

of desire
  and despair.

* * *

24

Mercury I

I discover
  a tiny droplet

of water
  on my

left palm.
  It had

welled up
  from

the artesian
  basin

beneath my skin.
  Like

spilt mercury,
  it shone

mischievously,
  the nape of

every globule
  frozen

like
  silver-ice.

I tried
  to shake it

off, but it
  had solidified.

Hard like
  crystalline

marble,
  but

transparent
  in its intent.

* * *

Eye Lash

A lone lash
  from

my eye-lid
  had disengaged

itself,
  its vision

now resting
  on the page

I'd scribbled on.
  It formed

an unintentional
  arc,

an odd gesture
  of a smile.

But this
  I am sure,

was
  an accident.

* * *

Mercury II

Water-mercury
  had lost

its centre,
  and gravity.

The melt
  now

clinging to
  the curve

of that thick
  lash,

unattached,
  available.

* * *

Archipelago

My body—
  a conundrum

labelled
  P.U.C.—

'patient
  with

unknown
  condition'—

playing havoc,
  undecided

whether
  to live

long
  or perish

young
  without notice.

Corpuscles,
  platelets —

all
  fragmented

by the melting
  heat,

icebergs
  glowing

like
  volcano —

an archipelago —
  addressless

and
  unmapped.

I am
  an exile

everywhere—
  within

my own self,
  in my own

country,
  in my

adopted
  homeland.

I am
  an outcast

even in
  the hospital

set in
  Harrow's

bucolic
  surburbia.

Democracy
  used,

misused, and
  re-used again

like ash
  providing fodder.

I act
  as fertilizer

to other's
  experiments

and profit,
  aid

in their
  own gain.

Seismic
  separators—

land
  from water,

flesh
  from bone,

white
  from red,

breath
  from death.

The green
  monitor

goes pale —
  its electric

energy
  drowned

in contaminated
  fluid.

I stand
  on an errant

outcrop
  of land —

a floating
  island

without future
  or anchor.

But I don't
  mind

such transitory
  freedom.

It is
  enough

for
  a dreamer.

My terrain
  is ever-shifting,

and I am glad
  not to

get caught in
  the quagmire

of poetry
  and pretence,

of ambition
  and intellect,

of life
  and death.

* * *

XI

CODA
VERTEBRAE

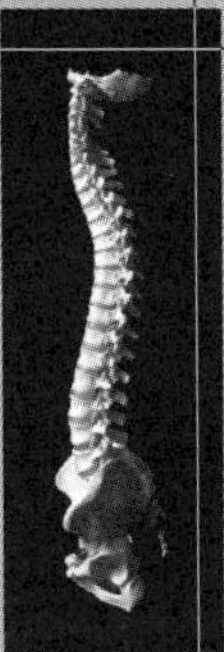

25

Break-Up

The spine—
  cervical,

thoracic,
  lumbar,

sacrum,
  coccyx—

all hold
  their

axis
  to form

an atlas
  that

provides
  relief

and
  posture,

anchoring
  the cord,

its humour
  and

human
  health.

* * *

Bone and
  bone

meet. Nerve-
  ends

make love.
  Synapse-

electricity
  magnetises

calcium
  transforming

child's
  palpability

to adult marrow-
  strength.

Carpal
  architecture

change their
  spine matrix —

thirty-three
  reduces to

twenty-six
  through

fusion's brittle
  maturation.

The rib-cage
  floats —

dozen-strung —
  subtly

held in
  moving space

by synovial's
  visible

and invisible
  juices,

and its fluid
  secrecy.

* * *

26

Coda

This thin
  country's

vertebrae,
  its own spine,

my
  archipelago,

geographies
  like locked

dactyls,
  distracted ...

* * *

... though
  oddly

connected,
  securing

the hold of
illusion

that allows us
to breathe,

safe
only in its

rising and
falling.

* * *

XII

AFTERWORD
THE JOURNEY & FORM

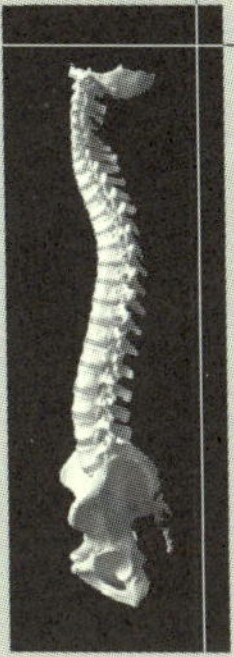

January, looking forward
and backward like the gatekeeper
god, was hot inside
and winter outside: first love
and lovers' quarrels.

A K RAMANUJAN, 'August'

The Journey & Form

And now we are moving on
like silent ships
not knowing where we've been
or where we're going, alone
in a world of pearls
and pitiless bricks.
— PABLO NERUDA

This piece began on a wet August morning in 1997, as I sat in a half-sunken basement space of a partially restored fifteenth century mansion 'Gartincaber' in Doune (near Stirling, Scotland). Drunk under the spell of this space, both interior and exterior, dactyls were dictated to me by the photons in surrounding electric-charged air—this was where my journey began.

My journey continued leaving a winding trail of footsteps, pug-marks I tried to hide, but could not. It is still an uncompleted journey, a journey that cannot be completed — perhaps due to one's own fallibility. This journey has infinitely long lines and many miles left to traverse, but I know my blood's inadequate crimson may prevent such an ambition. So I take all this as a gift, a dream — and feel constantly grateful that I have been allowed such a dream.

Along the way, I have been coloured and contaminated by many sources, interests, passions, and obsessions — some obvious and others oblique. Among them, there are overheard phrases, paintings, photographs, fragmented images, films, music, memory, poems, women, fluids, and the intoxicated air.

My alter ego wanted to be an architect and a cartographer — I have a more than part-time interest in science — all these must have, in some ways, influenced this piece.

I re-read many of my favourite poetry books at the time—classics like Milton's *Paradise Lost* and *Paradise Regained,* Rilke's *Duino Elegies,* and Baudelaire's *Fleur de Mal;* volumes by modern masters like Pablo Neruda, Octavio Paz, Joseph Brodsky, Seamus Heaney, Derek Walcott, and others.

Walcott's *Omeros,* Brodsky's *To Urania,* Galway Kinnell's *The Book of Nightmares,* Donald Hall's *The One Day,* Jaan Kaplinski's *The Same Sea In Us All,* Carole Maso's *Aureole,* Anne Michael's *Fugitive Pieces,* all of Michael Ondaatje's & Anne Carson's books, Arun Kolatkar's *Jejuri,* Dom Moraes's *Collected Poems, Serendip* & *In Cinnamon Shade,* Arvind Krishna Mehrotra's *Middle Earth,* A K Ramanujan's *Collected Poems,* especially kept me company. I have used fragments from many of these poets' work throughout the book (that appear in italics within the main text) to punctuate the narrative, so that readers can get some sense of their world as parallel asides, just as they did for me on my journey.

I was also immersed in Gray's *Anatomy,* Encarta's *BodyWorks,* Louis Kahn's *Sounds and Silence,* Matthew Arnold and T S Eliot's essays, John Frederick Nim's *Western Wind,* Edward Hirsch's *How to Read a Poem and Fall in Love with It,* and, Robert Pinsky's *Sound of Poetry.*

At the time, I relied on my grandfather's trusted old compass that helped navigate my way, imaginatively plotting a course through my *National Geographic* map collection that lay in disarray.

My memory provided calm, as I struggled, translating Jibanananda Das's 'Banalata Sen' from its Bengali original into English, to recreate its music and passion for a new tongue.

All of the above have been my guiding and travelling companions — and so the journey continued on —

The sparse elongated structure of this book-length piece reflects the strength and surety of the human vertebra and spine; much like Pablo Neruda's *Odes* that in turn reflect the long-thin shape of Chile. Sections and sub-sections join together like synapses between bone and bone. The titles are translucent markers or breath pauses — not separators.

The short two-line couplets echo the two-step footprints, a pathway that is mapped on an atlas. The 12 sections correspond to the 12 bones in a human ribcage, the 12 months in a year, the 12 hours in a day, and so on. There are 26 bones in the human vertebrae, and the 26 parts in the piece slowly assemble themselves to form a montage of tenuously strung lyrics. And finally, the 206 page-long work in this book match exactly the same number of bones in the human body.

This book has taken me 6 years to write — from its conception to completion. It is a piece that leaves footprints of a perennial walk that has meandered through public and private spaces — trying to make sense of the vicissitudes of one's loves, losses, wants, desires, and inadequacies — as it quietly continues to map the matrix of living and dying.

* * *

COLOPHON

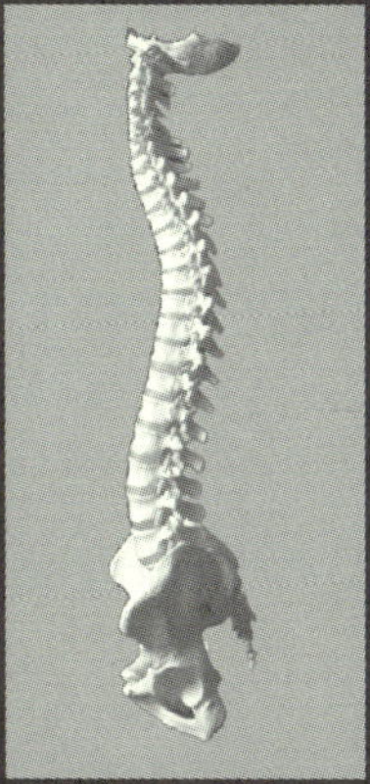

Acknowledgements

Many writers and critics have read and commented extensively on various versions of this book's manuscript — especially Kwame Dawes; the 'hypertext poetry workshop' gang — Kim Morrissey, Leona Medlin, Jane Draycott, Cahal Dallat, Hugh Epstein, Chris Hedley Dent, Elizabeth James, Duncan McGibbon, Richard Price & Peter Wyles; as well as Camille Lizarribar, Emma Neale & Paula Billbrough — to all of you, I owe a very big thank you.

My thanks are due to many doctors for their support at the Northwick Park Hospital in Harrow, a place that acted as my second home for many years and a place I continue to visit; thanks as well as to Dr Paul Nandi & Dr Raj Kapoor at the National Hospital for Neurology and Neurosurgery in Queen Square, London.

Grateful acknowledgments to the editors and producers who first published or broadcast parts of this book-length work, especially the ones at *The Literary Review, The Independent, Agenda, Cencrastus, Lines Review, Poetry Scotland, Van Gogh's Ear, World View, Prometeo, International Gallerie, The Little Magazine, Gentleman, The British Council Quarterly, The Daily Star, The News Today, Six Seasons Review, Aark Arts Review,* and, the *BBC.*

'Offering' appeared in *BodyText* (London,1999); and 'Ambassador' appeared in *Edinburgh: An Intimate City,* eds. B. Fraser & E. Grieg (Edinburgh, 2000). 'Kiss' won a commendation citation in the 2002 'Elsewhere: Back of Postcard Writing Competition' organized by Spread the Word, London — and appears in *Perpetual Diary* (London: Aark Arts).

Some of the erotic pieces in the section 'Passion' earlier appeared as a sequence in two separate limited edition chapbooks — [in English] *Lines of Desire* (USA: Triad/USC, 2000), and [in Spanish translation by Raul Jaime] *The Single Malt* (Medellin, Colombia: Prometeo, 2002).

My English translation of the Bengali original, 'Banalata Sen' by Jibanananda Das, first appeared in *In Another Tongue* (USA: Triad/USC, 2000), and, in *Agenda: Anthology of Poems & Translations,* eds. Anita Money & William Cookson (London, 1997).

'Graveyard' and 'The Journey & Form' appeared in *Poems & Sources,* edited by Thomas E Kennedy & Walter Cummins (New Jersey: Fairleigh Dickinson University, 2000), a commissioned volume that has contributions from 30 odd poets including—John Updike, Edwin Muir, Peter Mienke, Richard Jackson, Thomas Kinsella, Maxine Kumin, Albert Goldbarth, Carolyn Kizer, Eavan Boland, and Charles Simic.

I am also grateful to the Hawthornden Fellowship committee—the late Sir Stephen Spender, Christopher Reid, Jonathan Galassi, Adam Czernawski, and others—for awarding me an international writer's fellowship that enabled me to work on this manuscript in the peace and quiet of a Scottish Castle.

I fondly remember the company of my friends—fellow 'temporary sojourners' at Gartincaber mansion—Jeet [Thayil], Sudesh [Mishra], Elizabeth, Madelaine—a time when this piece was first born and played out in part.

In all the years of writing this book, my deepest love and gratitude to Priti & Aria for providing me with love and calm.

And finally, thanks to my American publisher Bryce Milligan of Wings Press, for his belief in my work and taking on such an avant-garde piece of work for a commercial market.

* * *

Publisher's Note

The publishers have made every effort to trace copyright holders, but in some cases without success. We shall be very glad to hear from anyone who has been inadvertently overlooked or incorrectly cited, and will make the necessary changes at the first opportunity.

* * *

About the Type

This book is set in Garamond — a typeface originally designed by the Parisian type cutter Claude Garamond (1480—1561). This version of Garamond was modelled on a 1592 specimen sheet from the Egenolff-Berner foundry, which was produced from types assumed to have been brought to Frankfurt by the punch cutter Jacques Sabon (d.1580).

Claude Garamond's distinguished romans and italics first appeared in *Opera Ciceronis* in 1543—44. The Garamond types are clear, open, and elegant.

* * *

About the Author

SUDEEP SEN [www.sudeepsen.com] was born in New Delhi in 1964 and studied literature there and the USA. As an Inlaks Scholar, he completed an MS from the Graduate School of Journalism at Columbia University in New York. He has written & edited over 25 books, including *Postmarked India: New & Selected Poems* (HarperCollins) — poems from which were awarded a Hawthornden Fellowship (UK) and a nominated for a Pushcart Prize (USA). Most recently, he has published *Postcards from Bangladesh, Monsoon,* and, *Revival.*

His writings have appeared in leading publcations, such as the *Times Literary Supplement, Guardian, Indipendent, Financial Times, London Magazine, Poetry Review, Literary Review, Haruard Review, Times of India, Statesman, Observer, Outlook, Gentleman, Biblio, Idian Review of Books,* among others.

As an invited author, he has read his work world-wide, won numerous awards, and has been translated into several languages including Bengali, Spanish, German, Italian, Greek, Hebrew, Persian, Romanian, Macedonian, Slovenian, Korean, and others.

Sen has been an international poet-in-residence at The Scottish Poetry Library and a visiting scholar at Harvard University.

Sudeep Sen is the editorial director of AARK ARTS, on the editorial board of *The Journal of Commonwealth Literature* and *Six Seasons Review,* and an associate of *The Paris Review.*

* * *

Works by Sudeep Sen

POETRY/FICTION
[Books & Chapbooks]
Leaning Against the Lamppost; The Lunar Visitations; Kali in Ottava Rima; New York Times; Parallel: Selected Poems; South African Woodcut; Mount Vesuvius in Eight Frames; Dali's Twisted Hands; Postmarked India: New & Selected Poems; BodyText; Retracing American Contours; Almanac; Lines of Desire; A Blank Letter; Perpetual Diary; Postcards from Bangladesh; Monsoon; The Single Malt; Revival; Distracted Geographies: An Archipelago of Intent

EDITOR/TRANSLATOR
[Books & Journals]
Lines Review Twelve Modern Young Indian Poets; Wasafiri Contemporary Writings from India, South Asia & the Diaspora; Index on Censorship Songs [Poems] of Partition; In Another Tongue; The British Council Book of Emerging English Poets from Bangladesh; Hayat Saif: Selected Poems; Love & Other Poems by Aminur Rahman; Dash: Four New German Writers; Modern English Poetry from Bangladesh; Aark Arts Review; Six Seasons Review

* * *

Wings Press Titles

FICTION, POETRY, DRAMA, ART, PHOTOGRAPHY, TEXTBOOK
(recent & forthcoming)

Barker, Wendy. *Way of Whiteness*
Bonazzi, Robert. *Fictive Music: Prose Poems 1975-1977*
Bourque, Darrell. .*Burnt Water Suite*
Crews, Judson. *nolo contendere [with a preface by Robert Creeley]*
Crockett, Eleanor Earle. *'53 Ford*
Dameron, Chip. *Hook & Bloodline*
De León, Greta. *Splintered Silences / Silencios Astillados*
Fowler, David Gene. *Briefcase*
Garcia-Zapata, Victoria. *Peace in the Corazón*
Guzmán, Celeste. *Cánde, te estoy llamando*
Hatch, Sheila Sánchez. *Guadalupe and the Kaleidoscopic Screamer*
Hatch, Sheila Sánchez. *Strong Box Heart*
Hall, Donald. *Winter Poems from Eagle Pond*
Hoggard, James. *Trotter Ross*
Lehmann, Ruth P.M. *Blessed Bastard: A Novel of Sir Galahad*
Lehmann, Winfred P., Esther Raizen, H.J.J. Hewitt. *Biblical Hebrew: An Analytical Introduction*
Lowry, Janet. *Thin Dimes*
Martin, Courtenay. *Seven Cigarette Story*
McGee, M. W. *Ambrosia Dancing at Mary's*
Milligan, Bryce. *Working The Stone*
Monsivaís, Carolina. *Somewhere Between Houston and El Paso*
Nye, Naomi Shihab. *Travel Alarm*
O'Loughlin, Raphael. *Basilian Leaders from Texas*
Philips, Robert. *Face to Face*
Pinson, Hermine. *Mama Yetta and Other Poems*
Pollentier, Nicole. *Smolt*
Rodriguez, Mary Grace. *Long story short*
Sen, Sudeep. *Revival: Poems & Translations 1983-2003*
Sen, Sudeep. *Distracted Geographies: An Archipelago of Intent*
Suárez, Virgil. *Garabato Poems*

Tafolla, Carmen. *Baby Coyote and the Old Woman*
Tafolla, Carmen. *Sonnets and Salsa*
Treviño, Frances Marie. *The Laughter of Doves*
Ushuk, Pamela. *Finding Peaches in the Desert*
Ventura, Michael. *The Mollyhawk Poems*
Ventura, Michael. *Sitting on Moving Steel*
Van Zandt, Townes. *For the Sake of the Song*

The first three hundred copies of
DISTRACTED GEOGRAPHIES: AN ARCHIPELAGO OF INTENT
by
SUDEEP SEN
to be pulled from the press as a limited edition
have been individually numbered,
signed, and dated by the author.

This copy is number:

____

____

Signed

____

Dated